Collins

Fractions and decimals

quick quizzes

Ages 7–9

$\dfrac{12}{100}$

6.6

$\dfrac{5}{8}$

78.4

Angela Smith

Recognising fractions

What fraction of each shape is coloured?

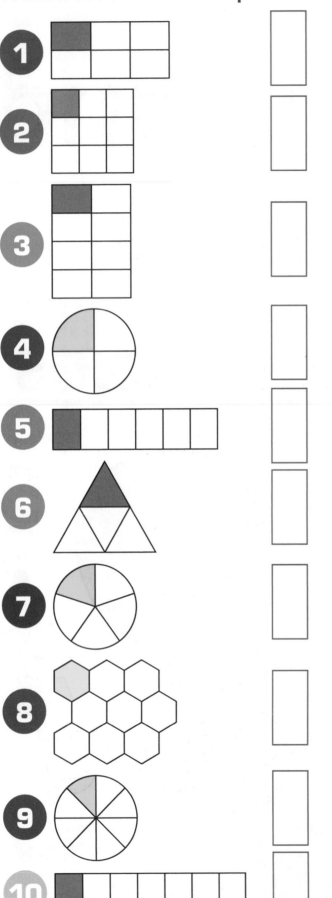

Colour your score

Unit fractions

Complete the number sentences.

1 $\frac{1}{3}$ of 18 = ☐

2 $\frac{1}{5}$ of 25 = ☐

3 $\frac{1}{2}$ of 28 = ☐

4 $\frac{1}{4}$ of 24 = ☐

5 $\frac{1}{10}$ of 40 = ☐

6 $\frac{1}{8}$ of 16 = ☐

7 $\frac{1}{7}$ of 35 = ☐

8 $\frac{1}{6}$ of 36 = ☐

9 $\frac{1}{9}$ of 27 = ☐

10 $\frac{1}{10}$ of 60 = ☐

11 $\frac{1}{4}$ of 32 = ☐

12 $\frac{1}{6}$ of 48 = ☐

13 $\frac{1}{8}$ of 32 = ☐

14 $\frac{1}{3}$ of 24 = ☐

15 $\frac{1}{5}$ of 45 = ☐

Divide the number by the denominator in the fraction.

15 14 13 12 11 10 9 8 7 6 5 4 3 1 2 1

Colour your score

Fractions of shapes

What fraction of each shape is coloured?

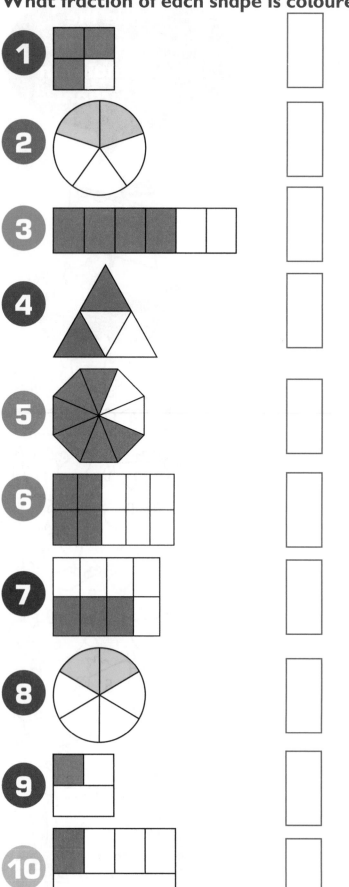

1

2

3

4

5

6

7

8

9

10

How many parts are there and how many are coloured?

Colour your score

4

Finding fractions

Colour each shape to show the fraction.

1 $\frac{4}{6}$

2 $\frac{6}{8}$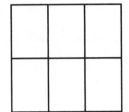

3 $\frac{6}{10}$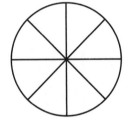

4 $\frac{4}{9}$

5 $\frac{3}{4}$

6 $\frac{7}{8}$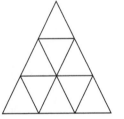

7 $\frac{1}{8}$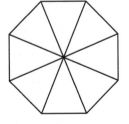

8 $\frac{1}{3}$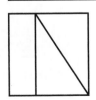

The numerator (top number) shows how many parts to colour.

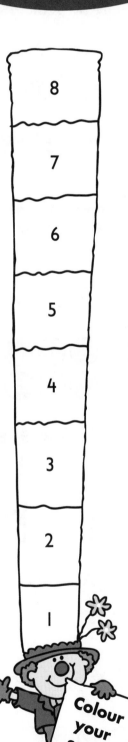

Colour your score

Fractions of sets

What fraction of each set is coloured?

1

2

3

4

5

6

7

8

9

10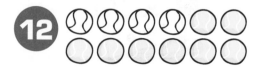

11

12

How many items are there and how many are coloured?

Colour your score

6

More fractions of sets

Colour the correct number of items to show the fraction.

1 $\frac{5}{6}$

2 $\frac{12}{16}$

3 $\frac{9}{10}$

4 $\frac{4}{5}$

5 $\frac{2}{3}$

6 $\frac{5}{9}$

7 $\frac{3}{7}$

8 $\frac{5}{10}$

9 $\frac{4}{6}$

10 $\frac{3}{4}$

11 $\frac{8}{10}$

12 $\frac{3}{5}$

Count the items and then decide how many to colour.

Colour your score

7

Fractions of numbers

Work out the amounts.

1 $\frac{3}{5}$ of 20 =

2 $\frac{4}{10}$ of 50 =

3 $\frac{3}{4}$ of 16 =

4 $\frac{6}{9}$ of 27 =

5 $\frac{4}{6}$ of 36 =

6 $\frac{3}{7}$ of 49 =

7 $\frac{8}{12}$ of 60 =

8 $\frac{4}{5}$ of 35 =

9 $\frac{7}{10}$ of 70 =

10 $\frac{3}{8}$ of 40 =

11 $\frac{8}{9}$ of 54 =

12 $\frac{2}{6}$ of 48 =

13 $\frac{5}{7}$ of 63 =

14 $\frac{10}{12}$ of 60 =

15 $\frac{7}{8}$ of 64 =

÷ by the denominator, then × by the numerator.

15 14 13 12 11 10 9 8 7 6 5 4 3 2 1

Colour your score

8

Comparing fractions

Fill in the box using < , > or = for each pair of fractions.

1 $\frac{1}{2}$ ☐ $\frac{1}{8}$

2 $\frac{1}{3}$ ☐ $\frac{1}{7}$

3 $\frac{1}{4}$ ☐ $\frac{1}{3}$

4 $\frac{1}{10}$ ☐ $\frac{1}{5}$

5 $\frac{5}{10}$ ☐ $\frac{1}{2}$

6 $\frac{1}{4}$ ☐ $\frac{1}{6}$

7 $\frac{2}{9}$ ☐ $\frac{7}{9}$

8 $\frac{3}{7}$ ☐ $\frac{2}{7}$

9 $\frac{6}{12}$ ☐ $\frac{5}{10}$

10 $\frac{1}{4}$ ☐ $\frac{1}{9}$

11 $\frac{1}{12}$ ☐ $\frac{1}{2}$

12 $\frac{6}{6}$ ☐ $\frac{5}{5}$

13 $\frac{5}{10}$ ☐ $\frac{5}{12}$

14 $\frac{1}{4}$ ☐ $\frac{6}{9}$

15 $\frac{1}{8}$ ☐ $\frac{1}{2}$

The more parts something is divided into, the smaller they will be.

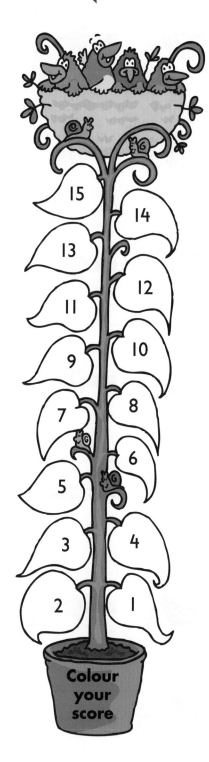

Colour your score

9

Simplifying fractions

Use the highest common factor (HCF) to simplify each fraction.

1 $\frac{2}{4}$ → ☐   **9** $\frac{4}{12}$ → ☐

2 $\frac{3}{9}$ → ☐   **10** $\frac{9}{12}$ → ☐

3 $\frac{2}{8}$ → ☐   **11** $\frac{6}{8}$ → ☐

4 $\frac{8}{12}$ → ☐   **12** $\frac{4}{8}$ → ☐

5 $\frac{2}{10}$ → ☐   **13** $\frac{6}{10}$ → ☐

6 $\frac{4}{6}$ → ☐   **14** $\frac{3}{12}$ → ☐

7 $\frac{6}{9}$ → ☐   **15** $\frac{5}{10}$ → ☐

8 $\frac{8}{10}$ → ☐

Use the highest number that both parts of the fraction can be divided by.

15
14
13
12
11
10
9
8
7
6
5
4
3
1 2

Colour your score

Equivalent fractions

Use a tick or cross to show if the fractions are equivalent.

Equivalent means 'equal'.

1. □

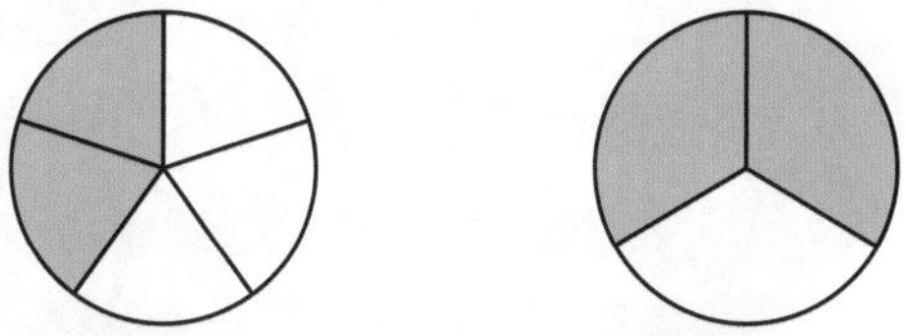

2. □

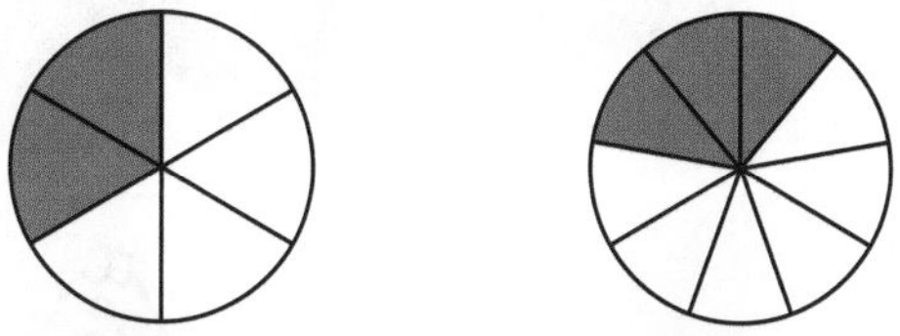

3. □

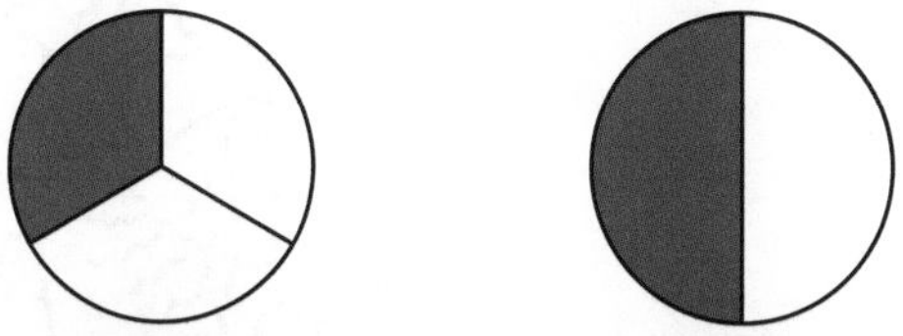

4. □

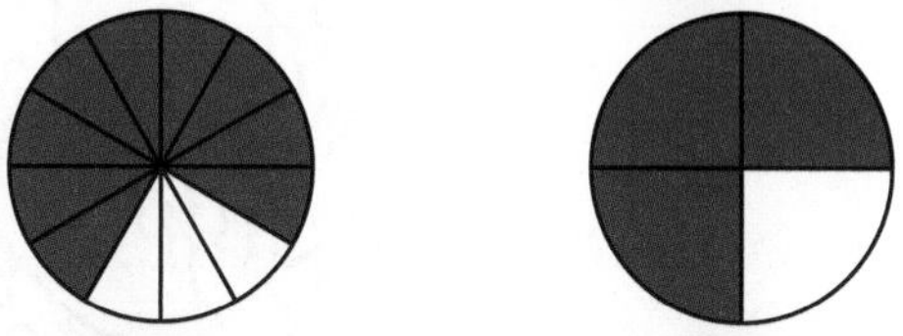

5. □

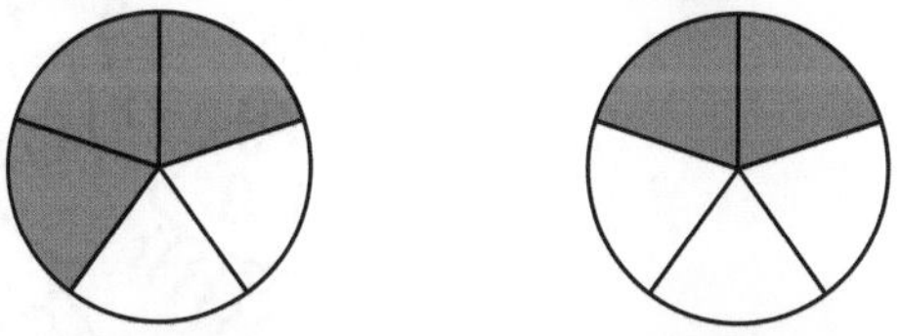

6. □

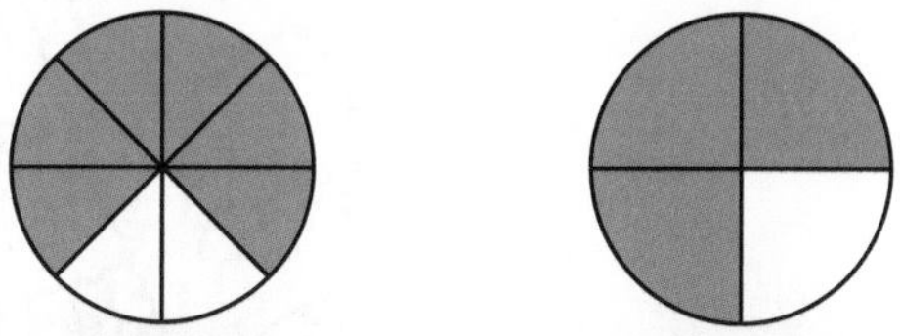

7. □

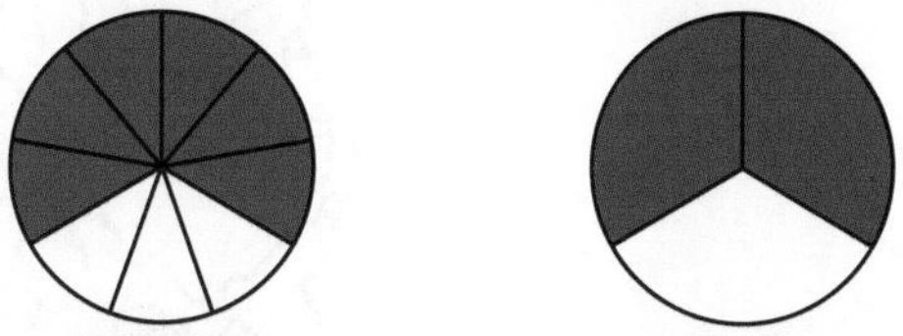

8. □

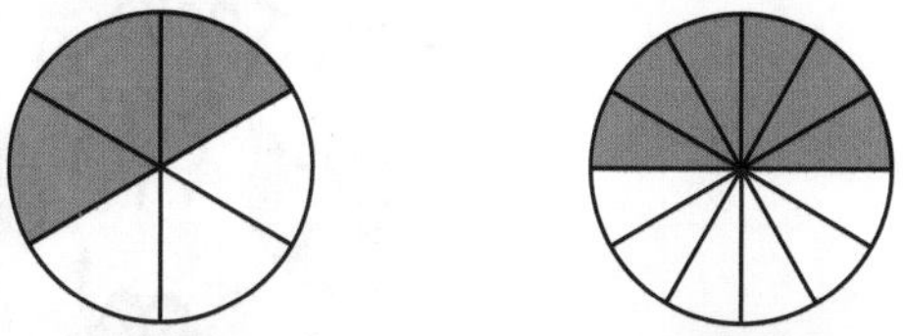

9. □

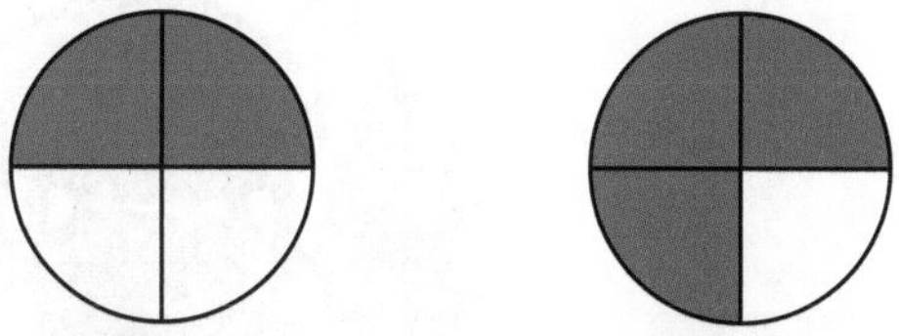

10. □

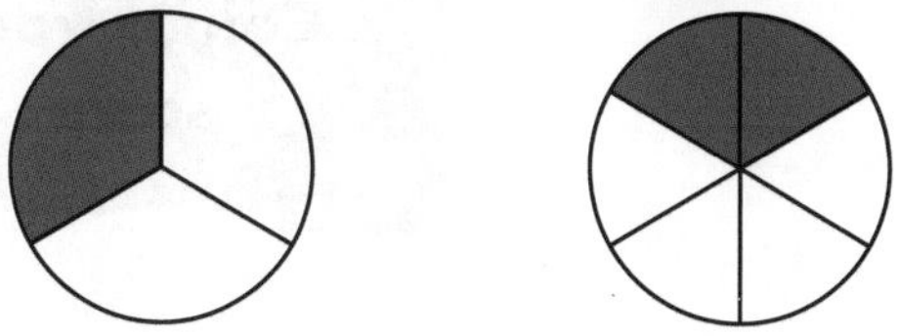

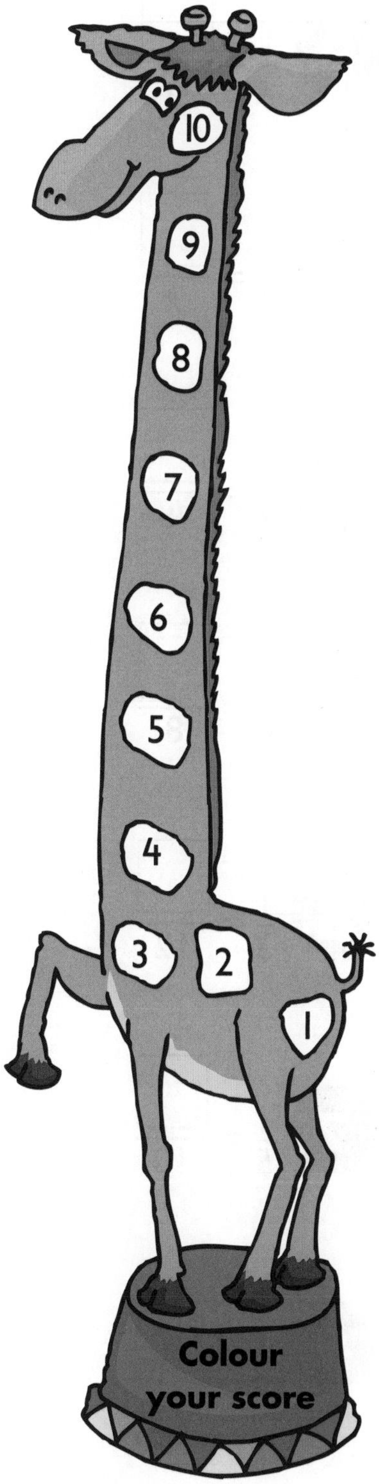

Colour your score

More equivalent fractions

Fill in the missing number to make an equivalent fraction.

1 $\dfrac{1}{2} = \dfrac{\boxed{}}{8}$

2 $\dfrac{1}{4} = \dfrac{\boxed{}}{12}$

3 $\dfrac{1}{3} = \dfrac{\boxed{}}{9}$

4 $\dfrac{1}{2} = \dfrac{\boxed{}}{4}$

5 $\dfrac{1}{4} = \dfrac{\boxed{}}{8}$

6 $\dfrac{1}{3} = \dfrac{\boxed{}}{12}$

7 $\dfrac{1}{5} = \dfrac{\boxed{}}{10}$

8 $\dfrac{1}{6} = \dfrac{2}{\boxed{}}$

9 $\dfrac{3}{4} = \dfrac{\boxed{}}{12}$

10 $\dfrac{2}{3} = \dfrac{\boxed{}}{9}$

11 $\dfrac{3}{5} = \dfrac{6}{\boxed{}}$

12 $\dfrac{3}{9} = \dfrac{\boxed{}}{3}$

13 $\dfrac{3}{12} = \dfrac{1}{\boxed{}}$

14 $\dfrac{8}{12} = \dfrac{\boxed{}}{3}$

15 $\dfrac{2}{6} = \dfrac{\boxed{}}{12}$

Multiply or divide the numerator and denominator by the same amount.

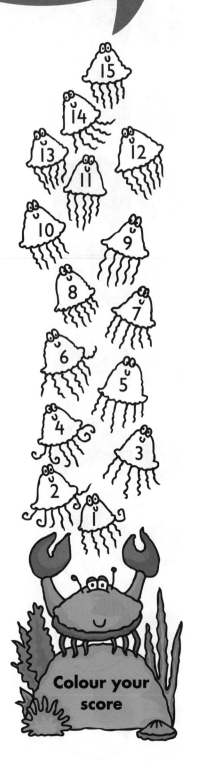

Colour your score

12

Ordering fractions

Put the fractions in order, smallest first.

1 $\frac{2}{8}$ $\frac{6}{8}$ $\frac{5}{8}$ $\frac{3}{8}$

2 $\frac{5}{9}$ $\frac{7}{9}$ $\frac{2}{9}$ $\frac{8}{9}$

3 $\frac{3}{7}$ $\frac{1}{7}$ $\frac{5}{7}$ $\frac{2}{7}$

4 $\frac{6}{12}$ $\frac{2}{12}$ $\frac{9}{12}$ $\frac{5}{12}$

5 $\frac{3}{10}$ $\frac{7}{10}$ $\frac{5}{10}$ $\frac{8}{10}$

6 $\frac{1}{2}$ $\frac{1}{8}$ $\frac{1}{5}$ $\frac{1}{4}$

7 $\frac{1}{4}$ $\frac{1}{3}$ $\frac{1}{9}$ $\frac{1}{7}$

8 $\frac{1}{3}$ $\frac{1}{9}$ $\frac{1}{10}$ $\frac{1}{2}$

9 $\frac{1}{6}$ $\frac{1}{8}$ $\frac{1}{10}$ $\frac{1}{4}$

10 $\frac{1}{5}$ $\frac{1}{7}$ $\frac{1}{10}$ $\frac{1}{2}$

For unit fractions, the bigger the denominator, the smaller the fraction.

Colour your score

13

Adding fractions

Add the following fractions.

1 $\dfrac{1}{6}$ + $\dfrac{3}{6}$ =   ☐

2 $\dfrac{2}{8}$ + $\dfrac{4}{8}$ =   ☐

3 $\dfrac{3}{10}$ + $\dfrac{5}{10}$ =   ☐

4 $\dfrac{2}{5}$ + $\dfrac{1}{5}$ =   ☐

5 $\dfrac{3}{12}$ + $\dfrac{5}{12}$ =   ☐

6 $\dfrac{2}{10}$ + $\dfrac{4}{10}$ + $\dfrac{3}{10}$ =   ☐

7 $\dfrac{2}{12}$ + $\dfrac{5}{12}$ + $\dfrac{3}{12}$ =   ☐

8 $\dfrac{3}{11}$ + $\dfrac{5}{11}$ + $\dfrac{2}{11}$ =   ☐

9 $\dfrac{3}{9}$ + $\dfrac{2}{9}$ + $\dfrac{3}{9}$ =   ☐

10 $\dfrac{2}{7}$ + $\dfrac{2}{7}$ + $\dfrac{3}{7}$ =   ☐

When fractions have the same denominator, just add the numerators.

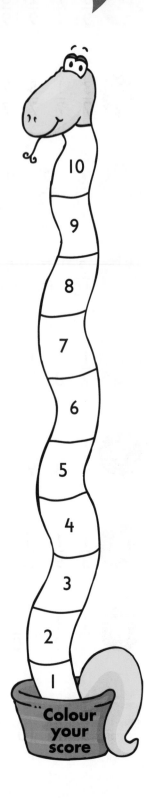

Colour your score

10
9
8
7
6
5
4
3
2
1

Subtracting fractions

Subtract the fractions.

1 $\frac{8}{9} - \frac{1}{9} =$ ☐

2 $\frac{7}{8} - \frac{5}{8} =$ ☐

3 $\frac{4}{5} - \frac{3}{5} =$ ☐

4 $\frac{8}{10} - \frac{5}{10} =$ ☐

5 $\frac{6}{8} - \frac{2}{8} =$ ☐

6 $\frac{9}{12} - \frac{4}{12} =$ ☐

7 $\frac{5}{7} - \frac{3}{7} =$ ☐

8 $\frac{7}{8} - \frac{2}{8} =$ ☐

9 $\frac{9}{10} - \frac{4}{10} =$ ☐

10 $\frac{7}{9} - \frac{4}{9} =$ ☐

11 $\frac{9}{8} - \frac{3}{8} =$ ☐

12 $\frac{9}{12} - \frac{5}{12} =$ ☐

13 $\frac{8}{10} - \frac{3}{10} =$ ☐

14 $\frac{7}{11} - \frac{3}{11} =$ ☐

15 $\frac{11}{12} - \frac{3}{12} =$ ☐

The denominator stays the same. Subtract the numerators only.

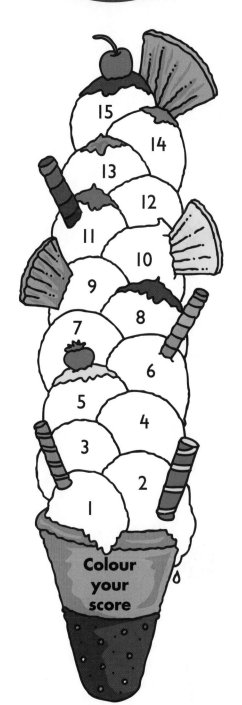

Colour your score

15

Decimal tenths

Draw a ring around the tenths digit in each decimal number.

1 2.7

2 6.5

3 6.9

4 8.5

5 7.6

6 5.8

7 9.6

8 12.4

9 9.63

10 15.21

11 27.60

12 56.40

13 127.64

14 329.70

15 685.98

The tenths digit is straight after the decimal point.

Colour your score

15
14
13
12
11
10
9
8
7
6
5
4
3
2
1

16

Continue the pattern

Count on or back in tenths to continue each sequence.

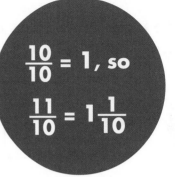

$\frac{10}{10} = 1$, so

$\frac{11}{10} = 1\frac{1}{10}$

1 $\frac{1}{10}$, $\frac{2}{10}$, $\frac{3}{10}$, _____, _____, _____

2 $\frac{5}{10}$, $\frac{6}{10}$, $\frac{7}{10}$, _____, _____, _____

3 1, $1\frac{1}{10}$, $1\frac{2}{10}$, _____, _____, _____

4 $1\frac{4}{10}$, $1\frac{5}{10}$, $1\frac{6}{10}$, _____, _____, _____

5 $\frac{9}{10}$, 1, $1\frac{1}{10}$, _____, _____, _____

6 $2\frac{8}{10}$, $2\frac{9}{10}$, 3, _____, _____, _____

7 $5\frac{6}{10}$, $5\frac{7}{10}$, $5\frac{8}{10}$, _____, _____, _____

8 $2\frac{1}{10}$, 2, $1\frac{9}{10}$, _____, _____, _____

9 $\frac{8}{10}$, $\frac{7}{10}$, $\frac{6}{10}$, _____, _____, _____

10 $4\frac{6}{10}$, $4\frac{5}{10}$, $4\frac{4}{10}$, _____, _____, _____

11 $\frac{6}{10}$, $\frac{5}{10}$, $\frac{4}{10}$, _____, _____, _____

12 $1\frac{2}{10}$, $1\frac{1}{10}$, 1, _____, _____, _____

13 $5\frac{9}{10}$, 6, $6\frac{1}{10}$, _____, _____, _____

14 $2\frac{3}{10}$, $2\frac{2}{10}$, $2\frac{1}{10}$, _____, _____, _____

15 $5\frac{4}{10}$, $5\frac{3}{10}$, $5\frac{2}{10}$, _____, _____, _____

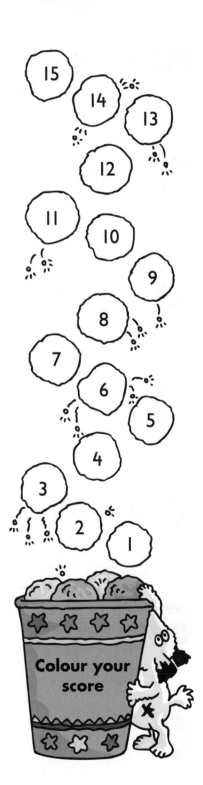

Colour your score

17

Tenths and hundredths

Write your answer as a fraction with 10 or 100 as the denominator.

1 $1 \div 10 = \boxed{}$

2 $4 \div 100 = \boxed{}$

3 $12 \div 100 = \boxed{}$

4 $2 \div 10 = \boxed{}$

5 $6 \div 10 = \boxed{}$

6 $25 \div 100 = \boxed{}$

7 $3 \div 10 = \boxed{}$

8 $7 \div 100 = \boxed{}$

9 $4 \div 10 = \boxed{}$

10 $10 \div 100 = \boxed{}$

11 $8 \div 10 = \boxed{}$

12 $62 \div 100 = \boxed{}$

13 $75 \div 100 = \boxed{}$

14 $16 \div 100 = \boxed{}$

15 $90 \div 100 = \boxed{}$

> $1 \div 10 = \frac{1}{10}$ and
> $1 \div 100 = \frac{1}{100}$

Colour your score

15 14 13 12 11 10 9 8 7 6 5 4 3 2 1

Fractions as decimals

Write each fraction as a decimal.

Look at the denominator!

1 $\frac{4}{10}$ ➡ 0._____

2 $\frac{3}{100}$ ➡ 0._____

3 $\frac{9}{10}$ ➡ 0._____

4 $\frac{7}{10}$ ➡ 0._____

5 $\frac{25}{100}$ ➡ 0._____

6 $\frac{5}{10}$ ➡ _____

7 $\frac{47}{100}$ ➡ _____

8 $\frac{62}{100}$ ➡ _____

9 $\frac{2}{10}$ ➡ _____

10 $\frac{52}{100}$ ➡ _____

11 $\frac{99}{100}$ ➡ _____

12 $\frac{1}{10}$ ➡ _____

13 $\frac{36}{100}$ ➡ _____

14 $\frac{8}{10}$ ➡ _____

15 $\frac{75}{100}$ ➡ _____

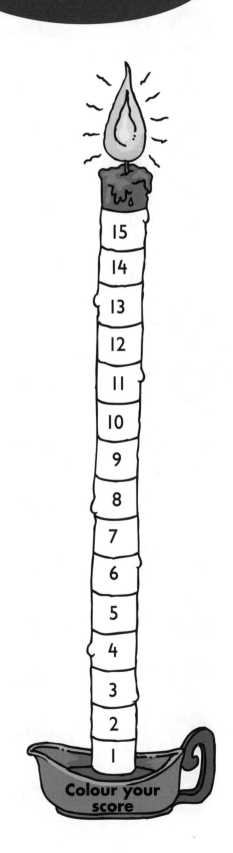

15
14
13
12
11
10
9
8
7
6
5
4
3
2
1

Colour your score

More fractions as decimals

Write these fractions as decimals.

1 $\frac{2}{10}$ ➡ 0._____

2 $\frac{13}{100}$ ➡ _____

3 $\frac{1}{10}$ ➡ _____

4 $\frac{18}{100}$ ➡ _____

5 $\frac{75}{100}$ ➡ _____

6 $\frac{39}{100}$ ➡ _____

7 $\frac{3}{10}$ ➡ _____

8 $\frac{42}{100}$ ➡ _____

9 $\frac{27}{100}$ ➡ _____

10 $\frac{4}{10}$ ➡ _____

11 $\frac{85}{100}$ ➡ _____

12 $\frac{98}{100}$ ➡ _____

13 $\frac{5}{10}$ ➡ _____

14 $\frac{6}{10}$ ➡ _____

15 $\frac{65}{100}$ ➡ _____

For fractions less than 1, put a zero before the decimal point.

Colour your score

20

Ordering decimals

Put these decimals in order of size, largest first.

Look for whole numbers first, then tenths, then hundredths.

1 0.3 0.6 0.1 0.8

_____ _____ _____ _____

2 0.02 0.01 0.06 0.09

_____ _____ _____ _____

3 0.58 0.61 0.42 0.37

_____ _____ _____ _____

4 0.28 0.11 0.63 0.82

_____ _____ _____ _____

5 0.03 0.31 0.13 0.10

_____ _____ _____ _____

6 5.03 5.13 5.23 5.33

_____ _____ _____ _____

7 0.25 kg 0.5 kg 0.42 kg

_____ _____ _____

8 3.26 m 3.53 m 3.62 m

_____ _____ _____

9 £0.62 £0.85 £0.88

_____ _____ _____

10 1.4 kg 1.62 kg 2.15 kg

_____ _____ _____

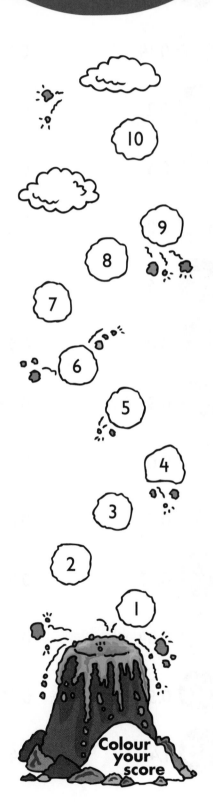

Colour your score

21

Comparing decimals

Circle the largest decimal in each pair.

Compare tenths first, then hundredths.

1   0.6   0.8

2   0.25   0.15

3   0.14   0.4

4   0.2   0.9

5   0.5   0.25

6   0.08   0.8

7   0.6   0.06

8   0.09   0.9

9   0.3   0.03

10   0.01   0.1

11   0.7   0.07

12   0.02   0.2

13   0.04   0.4

14   0.5   0.05

15   1.4   0.4

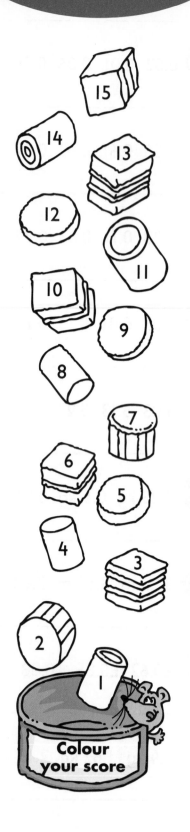

Colour your score

Number lines

Write the decimal shown by the arrow on each number line.

Some answers will be tenths, some hundredths.

1 0 ──────────────── 1

2 0 ──────────────── 1

3 0 ──────────────── 1

4 1 ──────────────── 2

5 1 ──────────────── 2

6 1 ──────────────── 2

7 0.1 ──────────────── 0.2

8 0.1 ──────────────── 0.2

9 0.1 ──────────────── 0.2

10 0.1 ──────────────── 0.2

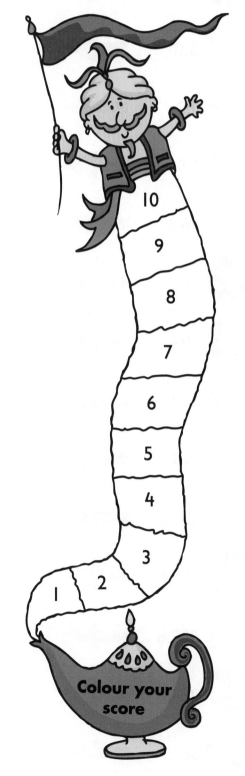

10
9
8
7
6
5
4
3
2
1

Colour your score

Rounding decimals

Round these decimals to the nearest whole number.

1 2.7 ➡️ ☐

2 4.1 ➡️ ☐

3 5.8 ➡️ ☐

4 7.2 ➡️ ☐

5 9.9 ➡️ ☐

6 14.6 ➡️ ☐

7 18.2 ➡️ ☐

8 19.4 ➡️ ☐

9 12.8 ➡️ ☐

10 17.1 ➡️ ☐

11 133.6 ➡️ ☐

12 427.1 ➡️ ☐

13 358.8 ➡️ ☐

14 296.4 ➡️ ☐

15 301.5 ➡️ ☐

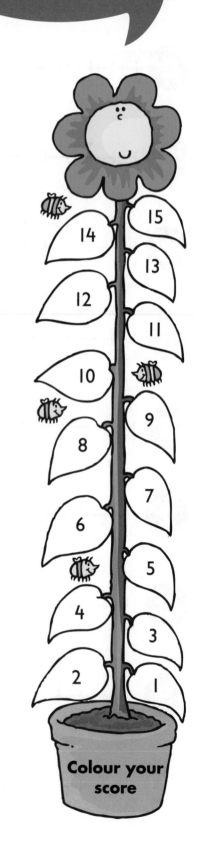

Colour your score

Decimal pairs

Circle two decimals in each set that add up to 1.

10 tenths make one whole.

1 0.6   0.3   0.4   0.5

2 0.1   0.8   0.2   0.4

3 0.1   0.3   0.9   0.6

4 0.3   0.7   0.5   0.8

5 0.22   0.12   0.78   0.87

6 0.18   0.84   0.19   0.81

7 0.51   0.32   0.49   0.70

8 0.65   0.35   0.25   0.55

9 0.83   0.73   0.37   0.17

10 0.01   0.04   0.99   0.89

11 0.09   0.92   0.94   0.08

12 0.15   0.65   0.75   0.25

13 0.42   0.41   0.58   0.55

14 0.03   0.93   0.05   0.97

15 0.24   0.29   0.71   0.77

Colour your score

Adding decimals

Add these decimals.

1
```
    3 . 5
+   2 . 3
─────────
        .
```

2
```
    6 . 1
+   2 . 7
─────────
```

3
```
    3 . 5
+   4 . 2
─────────
```

4
```
  1 5 . 2
+ 1 1 . 6
─────────
```

5
```
  1 2 . 4
+ 1 3 . 5
─────────
```

6
```
  2 3 . 6
+ 2 4 . 4
─────────
```

7
```
  4 2 . 5
+ 4 2 . 5
─────────
```

8
```
    3 . 2 7
+   2 . 3 1
───────────
```

9
```
    5 . 3 2
+   3 . 6 4
───────────
```

10
```
  7 2 . 3 0
+ 1 9 . 4 2
───────────
```

11
```
  5 5 . 5 0
+ 2 3 . 6 0
───────────
```

12
```
  1 0 . 2 6
+ 1 3 . 5 4
───────────
```

13
```
  1 2 . 3 7
+ 1 5 . 8 1
───────────
```

14
```
  1 4 . 5 2
+ 1 1 . 5 6
───────────
```

Add decimals like whole numbers, but remember the decimal point.

Colour your score

Subtracting decimals

Subtract the decimals.

1
```
    6 . 8
 −  1 . 4
 _____
        .
```

2
```
    9 . 9
 −  2 . 6
 _____
```

3
```
    4 . 7
 −  1 . 5
 _____
```

4
```
  1 3 . 6
 −1 2 . 4
 _____
```

5
```
  1 8 . 9
 −1 0 . 3
 _____
```

6
```
  5 7 . 4
 −3 3 . 2
 _____
```

7
```
  2 4 . 6
 −1 2 . 8
 _____
```

8
```
  3 7 . 2 0
 −1 3 . 5 0
 _____
```

9
```
  2 3 . 2 8
 −1 5 . 1 4
 _____
```

10
```
  2 9 . 5 8
 −1 0 . 2 6
 _____
```

11
```
  3 4 . 9 5
 −2 3 . 7 4
 _____
```

12
```
  5 6 . 2 5
 −3 3 . 1 7
 _____
```

13
```
  6 4 . 5 4
 −2 3 . 2 6
 _____
```

14
```
  7 6 . 8 4
 −3 2 . 6 6
 _____
```

Subtract decimals like whole numbers, but remember the decimal point.

Colour your score

Dividing by 10 or 100

Divide these numbers by 10 or 100.

The digits will move 1 or 2 places to the right.

1 8 ÷ 10 =

2 6 ÷ 10 =

3 2 ÷ 10 =

4 7 ÷ 10 =

5 9 ÷ 10 =

6 16 ÷ 10 =

7 23 ÷ 10 =

8 49 ÷ 10 =

9 50 ÷ 10 =

10 7 ÷ 100 =

11 3 ÷ 100 =

12 9 ÷ 100 =

13 44 ÷ 100 =

14 82 ÷ 100 =

15 97 ÷ 100 =

Colour your score

Decimals to fractions

Convert these decimals into fractions.

Give your answers in the simplest form.

Convert to tenths or hundredths first.

1. 0.8 → ☐
2. 0.2 → ☐
3. 0.02 → ☐
4. 0.05 → ☐
5. 0.9 → ☐
6. 0.09 → ☐
7. 0.4 → ☐
8. 0.5 → ☐
9. 0.07 → ☐
10. 0.35 → ☐
11. 0.60 → ☐
12. 0.25 → ☐
13. 0.75 → ☐
14. 0.1 → ☐
15. 0.01 → ☐

15
14
13
12
11
10
9
8
7
6
5
4
3
2
1
Colour your score

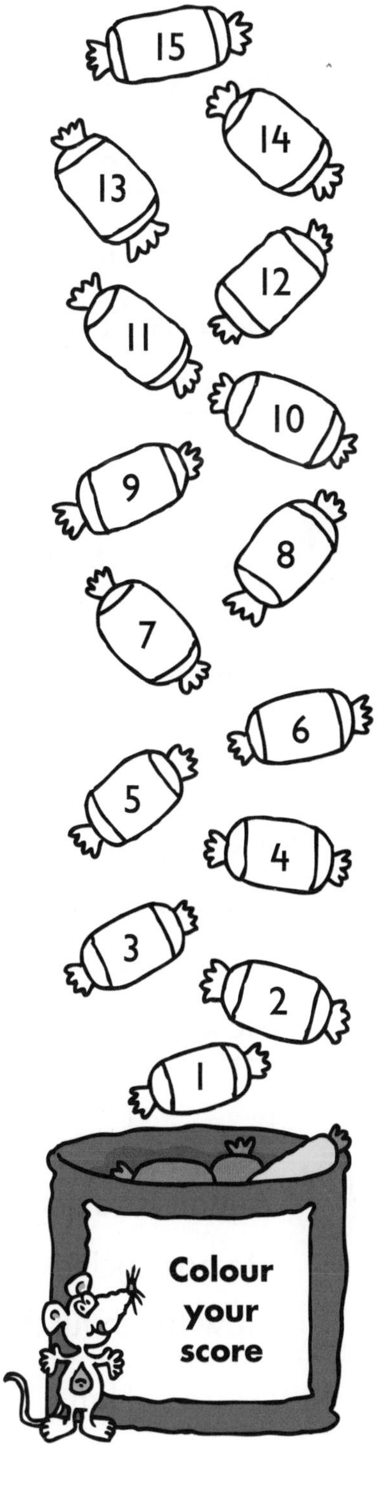

Fraction problems

Solve each problem and give your
answer as a number.

Underline
important numbers
and facts to help decide
which operation
to use.

1 Neil had £9. He spent $\frac{1}{3}$ on a DVD.
How much did he spend?

£ [ ]

2 A large chocolate cake weighs 800 g.
How much does $\frac{3}{4}$ of the cake weigh?

[ ] g

3 Mr. Jones has saved £900.
He uses $\frac{8}{10}$ to pay for a holiday.
How much does he have left to spend?

£ [ ]

4 There are 600 marbles in a jar.
$\frac{2}{5}$ are red. The rest are blue.
How many blue marbles are there?

[ ] blue marbles

5 There are 300 children in a school.
$\frac{2}{3}$ eat school dinners.
The rest eat packed lunches.
How many children eat packed lunches?

[ ] children

6 Ayaan is taking part in a 480 km cycling race.
He has cycled $\frac{3}{4}$ of the distance.
How much further does he have to go?

[ ] km

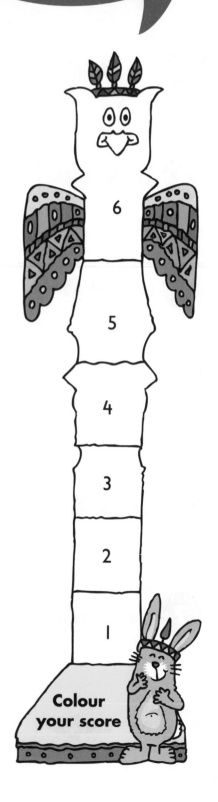

6

5

4

3

2

1

Colour
your score

Decimal problems

Solve these real life problems.

1 A piece of string is 7.6 m long.
3.9 m is cut off the end.
How much string is left?

[   ] m

2 Ben is 1.75 m tall.
His sister is 0.6 m shorter than him.
How tall is his sister?

[   ] m

3 A comic costs £1.65.
How much change will I get from £5?

£ [   ]

4 Lalia cycled 24.6 km in the morning and
12.8 km in the afternoon.
How far did she cycle altogether?

[   ] km

5 A pan holds 1.6 litres of soup.
Sam pours out 0.85 litres.
How much is still in the pan?

[   ] litres

6 One week, Mr. Smith collects 32.74 kg of
recycling waste.
The next week he collects 42.85 kg.
How much has he collected altogether?

[   ] kg

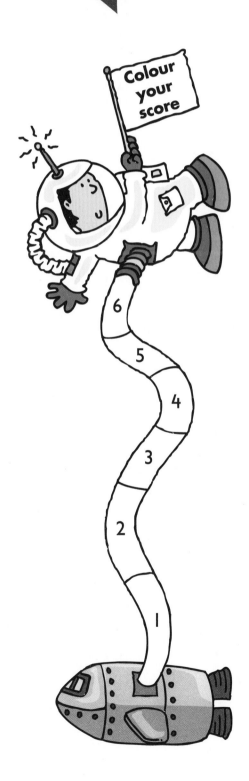

Underline numbers and important facts to help decide which operation to use.

Colour your score

6
5
4
3
2
1

Answers

Recognising fractions

1. $\frac{1}{6}$ 6. $\frac{1}{4}$
2. $\frac{1}{9}$ 7. $\frac{1}{5}$
3. $\frac{1}{8}$ 8. $\frac{1}{9}$
4. $\frac{1}{4}$ 9. $\frac{1}{8}$
5. $\frac{1}{6}$ 10. $\frac{1}{7}$

Unit fractions

1. 6   9. 3
2. 5   10. 6
3. 14   11. 8
4. 6   12. 8
5. 4   13. 4
6. 2   14. 8
7. 5   15. 9
8. 6

Fractions of shapes

1. $\frac{3}{4}$ 6. $\frac{4}{10}$ or $\frac{2}{5}$
2. $\frac{2}{5}$ 7. $\frac{3}{8}$
3. $\frac{4}{6}$ or $\frac{2}{3}$ 8. $\frac{2}{6}$ or $\frac{1}{3}$
4. $\frac{2}{4}$ or $\frac{1}{2}$ 9. $\frac{1}{4}$
5. $\frac{6}{8}$ or $\frac{3}{4}$ 10. $\frac{1}{8}$

Finding fractions

The following number of parts should be shaded:

1. 4
2. 6
3. 6
4. 4
5. 3
6. 7
7. 1 part in top section of rectangle ($\frac{1}{8}$)
8. 1

Fractions of sets

1. $\frac{2}{5}$ 7. $\frac{8}{10}$ or $\frac{4}{5}$
2. $\frac{3}{4}$ 8. $\frac{4}{8}$ or $\frac{1}{2}$
3. $\frac{6}{9}$ or $\frac{2}{3}$ 9. $\frac{2}{6}$ or $\frac{1}{3}$
4. $\frac{4}{6}$ or $\frac{2}{3}$ 10. $\frac{7}{10}$
5. $\frac{2}{3}$ 11. $\frac{3}{9}$ or $\frac{1}{3}$
6. $\frac{6}{12}$ or $\frac{1}{2}$ 12. $\frac{8}{12}$ or $\frac{2}{3}$

More fractions of sets

The following number of objects should be coloured:

1. 5   7. 3
2. 12   8. 5
3. 9   9. 4
4. 4   10. 3
5. 2   11. 8
6. 5   12. 3

Fractions of numbers

1. 12   9. 49
2. 20   10. 15
3. 12   11. 48
4. 18   12. 16
5. 24   13. 45
6. 21   14. 50
7. 40   15. 56
8. 28

Comparing fractions

1. >   9. =
2. >   10. >
3. <   11. <
4. <   12. =
5. =   13. >
6. >   14. <
7. <   15. <
8. >

Simplifying fractions

1. $\frac{1}{2}$ 9. $\frac{1}{3}$
2. $\frac{1}{3}$ 10. $\frac{3}{4}$
3. $\frac{1}{4}$ 11. $\frac{3}{4}$
4. $\frac{2}{3}$ 12. $\frac{1}{2}$
5. $\frac{1}{5}$ 13. $\frac{3}{5}$
6. $\frac{2}{3}$ 14. $\frac{1}{4}$
7. $\frac{2}{3}$ 15. $\frac{1}{2}$
8. $\frac{4}{5}$

Equivalent fractions

1. ✗   6. ✓
2. ✓   7. ✓
3. ✗   8. ✓
4. ✓   9. ✗
5. ✗   10. ✓

More equivalent fractions

1. $\frac{4}{8}$ 9. $\frac{9}{12}$
2. $\frac{3}{12}$ 10. $\frac{6}{9}$
3. $\frac{3}{9}$ 11. $\frac{6}{10}$
4. $\frac{2}{4}$ 12. $\frac{1}{3}$
5. $\frac{2}{8}$ 13. $\frac{1}{4}$
6. $\frac{4}{12}$ 14. $\frac{2}{3}$
7. $\frac{2}{10}$ 15. $\frac{4}{12}$
8. $\frac{2}{12}$

Ordering fractions

1. $\frac{2}{8}, \frac{3}{8}, \frac{5}{8}, \frac{6}{8}$
2. $\frac{2}{9}, \frac{5}{9}, \frac{7}{9}, \frac{8}{9}$
3. $\frac{1}{7}, \frac{2}{7}, \frac{3}{7}, \frac{5}{7}$
4. $\frac{2}{12}, \frac{5}{12}, \frac{6}{12}, \frac{9}{12}$
5. $\frac{3}{10}, \frac{5}{10}, \frac{7}{10}, \frac{8}{10}$
6. $\frac{1}{8}, \frac{1}{5}, \frac{1}{4}, \frac{1}{2}$
7. $\frac{1}{9}, \frac{1}{7}, \frac{1}{4}, \frac{1}{3}$
8. $\frac{1}{10}, \frac{1}{9}, \frac{1}{3}, \frac{1}{2}$
9. $\frac{1}{10}, \frac{1}{8}, \frac{1}{6}, \frac{1}{4}$
10. $\frac{1}{10}, \frac{1}{7}, \frac{1}{5}, \frac{1}{2}$

Adding fractions

1. $\frac{4}{6}$ or $\frac{2}{3}$ 6. $\frac{9}{10}$
2. $\frac{6}{8}$ or $\frac{3}{4}$ 7. $\frac{10}{12}$ or $\frac{5}{6}$
3. $\frac{8}{10}$ or $\frac{4}{5}$ 8. $\frac{10}{11}$
4. $\frac{3}{5}$ 9. $\frac{8}{9}$
5. $\frac{8}{12}$ or $\frac{2}{3}$ 10. $\frac{7}{7}$ or 1

Subtracting fractions

1. $\frac{7}{9}$ 9. $\frac{5}{10}$ or $\frac{1}{2}$
2. $\frac{2}{8}$ or $\frac{1}{4}$ 10. $\frac{3}{9}$ or $\frac{1}{3}$
3. $\frac{1}{5}$ 11. $\frac{6}{8}$ or $\frac{3}{4}$
4. $\frac{3}{10}$ 12. $\frac{4}{12}$ or $\frac{1}{3}$
5. $\frac{4}{8}$ or $\frac{1}{2}$ 13. $\frac{5}{10}$ or $\frac{1}{2}$
6. $\frac{5}{12}$ 14. $\frac{4}{11}$
7. $\frac{2}{7}$ 15. $\frac{8}{12}$ or $\frac{2}{3}$
8. $\frac{5}{8}$